# The Mediterranean Cookbook

## Jenna Watson

# Table of Contents

Introduction ................................................................................ 5

Chapter 1 – Getting Started on the Mediterranean Diet............................. 6

Chapter 2 – Mediterranean Seven Day Meal Plan .................................... 11

Chapter 3 – Breakfast Recipes ........................................................... 15

Sunny Side Up Eggs over Herbed Mushrooms.................................. 15

Garlic, Basil and Gruyere Cheese Scramble ..................................... 17

Italian Basil, Tomato and Asparagus Omelette.................................. 18

Breakfast Burritos of Roasted Red Pepper and Mackerel...................... 20

Baked Sausage and Vegetable Frittata............................................. 22

No Crust Greek Style Cheesy Spinach Quiche ................................... 24

No Crust Cheesy Broccoli and Tarragon Quiche................................. 26

Shakshuka ............................................................................... 28

Chapter 4 –Salads........................................................................... 30

Arugula, Fig and Prosciutto Salad with Walnut and Parmesan ............... 30

Greek Sardine and Garden Salad .................................................. 32

Pear and Arugula Salad with Apricot Vinaigrette, Almonds and Goat
Cheese .................................................................................... 34

Spiced Egg and Spinach Salad...................................................... 36

Red Pepper, Asparagus and Spinach Salad with Goat Cheese ................ 38

Hot Cauliflower and Feta Salad with Herbed Dressing ......................... 40

Radicchio, Date, and Citrus Salad with Smoked Almonds..................... 42

Moroccan Chili Tomato Salad ...................................................... 44

Asparagus, Orange and Hazelnut Pesto Salad with Feta ........................... 46

Zesty Fennel and Romaine Lettuce Salad ................................................. 48

Brussels Sprouts and Pecorino Salad with Pine Nuts ............................... 50

Green Beans, Onions and Ham Salad ...................................................... 51

Peppery Greens and Olive Salad with Feta Cheese .................................. 53

Classic Caponata ................................................................................... 54

Classic Nicoise Salad ............................................................................ 56

Chapter 5 – Light Soups ........................................................................ 59

Sicilian Escarole and Chickpea Soup ...................................................... 59

Italian Spinach, Parmesan and Brown Rice Soup ..................................... 61

Moroccan Tomato Soup .......................................................................... 63

Spiced Fava Bean Soup .......................................................................... 65

Turkish Bulgur, Red Pepper and Tomato Soup ........................................ 67

Chapter 6 – Seafood Main Dishes .......................................................... 69

Provence Style Fish Soup ....................................................................... 69

Shrimp, Celery, Leek and Fennel Soup ................................................... 71

Golden Leek and Shellfish Soup ............................................................. 73

Broiled Mackerel with Lemon and Israeli Green Hot Sauce ...................... 75

Braised Halibut with Dijon Mustard Leeks .............................................. 77

Herbed Lemon Haddock Fillets with Garlic Potatoes ............................... 79

Saffron Hake Soup with Potatoes and Chorizo ........................................ 81

Braised Cod with Coriander and Carrots ................................................. 83

Pan Roasted Striped Cod with Chermoula Sauce ..................................... 85

Braised Cod with Tarragon Fennel .......................................................... 87

Grilled Mackerel with Marjoram and Lemon ........................................... 89

Grilled Herring with Fennel and Orange .................................................. 91

Grilled Mackerel with Lime and Coriander ................................................ 93

Chapter 7 – Meat Main Dishes ...................................................... 95

Spanish Style Saffron and Pork Meatball Soup ........................................ 95

Grilled Tender Chicken Kebabs with Tomato and Feta Salad ................. 97

Oven Roasted Chicken Thighs with Fennel, Orange and Olive Sauce ..... 99

Oven Roasted Chicken Thighs with Moroccan Style Currant and Pistachio Sauce ........................................................................................... 101

Chicken Saute with Romesco Sauce ......................................................... 103

Spicy Moroccan Lamb and Lentil Stew .................................................... 105

Libyan Lamb and Mint Sharba ................................................................ 107

Chapter 8 – Snacks and Light Meals .......................................... 109

Pita Bread .................................................................................................. 109

Savory Chickpea Flatbread ....................................................................... 111

Spanish Chili Garlic Mushrooms ............................................................. 113

Goat Cheese and Roasted Bell Pepper Dip .............................................. 114

Green Olive and Lentil Dip ...................................................................... 115

Conclusion ........................................................................................ 117

# Introduction

When it comes to delicious and healthy food, it is hard to beat the reputation of the Mediterranean Diet. Not only is it rich in vegetables, fruits, seafood, legumes, and whole grains, it also calls for herbs, spices, olive oil, wine, and other ingredients packed full of flavour, aromas, and antioxidants. So, if you are looking for recipes to help you recreate some of the best Mediterranean dishes at home, then this book is definitely for you.

In this book you will read about how you can get started on the Mediterranean diet. Then, you will jump straight into practice as much of this book is dedicated to Mediterranean dish recipes.

To maximize this book, it is best for you to start by reading the first chapter. That way, you will find out how you can make this diet sustainable and enjoyable for yourself and your family throughout your life.

Then, you can jump right ahead to the recipes, or you can choose to use one of the seven all-day menus found in Chapter 2. If you plan on making the Mediterranean diet a part of your lifestyle, then it is best for you to follow the suggested menus in Chapter 2. However, you can always flip to the Table of Contents and choose the recipes you want between Chapters 3 to 8 to recreate for the day.

So, are you ready to begin your journey as a Mediterranean cook? Head on over to Chapter 1 to start now.

# Chapter 1 – Getting Started on the Mediterranean Diet

It might be close to impossible to describe the Mediterranean diet in a single chapter. This is especially due to the fact that the Mediterranean is composed of diverse countries, including Italy, northern Spain, France, Turkey, Greece, Israel, Lebanon, eastern Syria, Egypt, Morocco, Libya, Tunisia, and Algeria. Be that as it may, the diets of these different places have commonalities that give the world-known "Mediterranean" diet its unique blend of flavors, textures, and charm.

One of the most distinct features of the diet is its richness in terms of vegetables, beans, lentils, whole grains, seafood and, of course, olive oil. The meals of each day should be made up mostly of these foods, and it is due to this reason that the diet is known for being extremely healthy.

In fact, one study conducted by American scientist Dr. Ancel Keys in that 1950s revealed that the relatively socio-economically poor of the southern Italy have significantly longer lives and have a lower risk of developing heart disease, compared to the wealthy New Yorkers, mainly because of their diet.

Moreover, the natives rarely consume red meats such as beef, lamb, and pork because these commodities are considered expensive and thus a luxury. The same thing goes for sweets and other sugary treats, which are only enjoyed in special occasions. Wine and olive oil, however, being locally produced and abundant, are enjoyed in moderate portions. As wine contains the antioxidant *resveratrol* and olive oil *phenols, vitamin E,* which are known for their heart-healthy and anti-aging properties, these may also contribute to the health of the Mediterranean people.

Aside from maintaining this vegetable- and seafood-rich diet, the natives are also always physically active, whether it is fishing, farming, or gardening. Therefore, to gain the full health benefits of the diet it is essential for you to also incorporate regular exercise into your routine. Small changes such as taking the stairs over using the elevator, doing some early morning stretches, and taking 10 minute walks each day can spell a huge difference.

Now, with all these in mind here are some guidelines on how to get started on this wonderfully delicious yet incredibly healthy diet:

**Get rid of all processed foods**

If you start to look at processed foods as similar to drinking alcohol excessively or chain smoking, then you might be less likely to pick up your next bag of chips or bar of chocolate milk.

Processed foods are stuffed with chemicals, simple sugars, and sodium, all of which contribute substantially to the development of type 2 diabetes, obesity, atherosclerosis, and other debilitating diseases. Refined sugar, in particular, is often regarded as a "cancer feeder" because it facilitates the development of cancer tumors.

So, before you begin your diet you should get rid of all processed foods from your home. These include packaged snacks, boxed cereals, microwave meals, heavy meat products, cakes, biscuits, and so on.

Once you get rid of processed food, you can then proceed to fill your kitchen with the staple ingredients necessary to maintain the Mediterranean diet.

**Purchase high quality Mediterranean Diet staples**

Some of the ingredients you will frequently be using in preparing the recipes in this cookbook are as follows:

- Extra virgin olive oil
- Olive oil (for cooking)
- Nuts, seeds, and legumes (especially garbanzo beans or chickpeas, lentils, pistachios and almonds)
- Whole wheat and chickpea flours
- Garlic
- Onion and shallots
- Lemons, oranges and limes
- Honey (preferably pure raw)
- Ginger
- Turmeric (fresh and/or ground)
- Cinnamon (sticks and/or ground)
- Tarragon, Basil, Oregano (fresh and/or ground)
- Mint (fresh and/or dried)
- Parsley (fresh and/or dried)
- Sea salt (preferably Mediterranean pink salt)
- Freshly cracked/ground black pepper
- Red pepper flakes
- Olives

Of course, you do not have to purchase these all at once. Rather, you can gradually build upon your collection as you prepare each dish. You can actually save a lot as well if you grow your own herbs. Most, if not all, of the herbs listed above are quite easy to grow on your kitchen sill or in a pot in your backyard garden.

## Source from reliable local vegetable and seafood markets

As explained earlier, you will be eating lots of vegetables, whole grains, and seafood when you are on the Mediterranean diet. Therefore, it should come as to no surprise that you will be buying plenty of these types of foods. However, the only way for this to be sustainable is if you can find sources that consistently provide quality ingredients for your Mediterranean diet meals.

You can start with your local farmer's market and fishmonger. You can also ask your friends and family if they know markets that sell freshly caught fish and newly harvested vegetables. Talk to the vendors as well, to find out what is in season so that you can prioritize purchasing those. In season and locally available produce are not just cheaper, but better quality as well because they are much fresher.

## Choose a recipe and prepare it

Now, with everything in place all you need to do next is prepare your first Mediterranean dish. Choose a recipe containing ingredients that are readily available to you (or whose substitutes you can easily find in your area), calling for equipment you already have in the kitchen, and instructing steps that are not difficult for you to follow. After that, take note of the ingredients you need to prepare. Then, purchase them and get started! Just make sure to read the entire recipe before you start the fire.

There are plenty of recipes to choose from. You can whip up any one of the delectable Mediterranean breakfast recipes and serve your dish alongside black coffee or freshly squeezed orange or lemon juice. Before lunch, you might want to prepare one salad or soup as an appetizer or energizer later in the morning. For lunch, you can choose to serve either a seafood-or a meat-based main dish. Keep in mind, though, that you should limit the number of servings of red meat per week, as in the Mediterranean people rarely eat those. For a snack, you might want to prepare a special Mediterranean bread and then accompany it with a spread. Then, for dinner, you can go light or heavy depending on your fitness goals and whim.

As you can see, it is quite easy to get started on the Mediterranean diet, or at least enjoy delicious exotic meals every once in a while. In fact, you can get started right now. A wide array of choices is waiting for you ahead.

# Chapter 2 – Mediterranean Seven Day Meal Plan

Most likely you picked up this book because you want to start and maintain the Mediterranean diet, and that you would prefer to cook at home because – let's face it – good quality restaurant food is expensive. So, to help you begin your journey towards this healthier lifestyle, here are some suggested menus you can follow for the next seven days.

Keep in mind that you can always substitute certain ingredients with ones that are locally produced, in season, abundant, and cheap in your area. You can also come up with your own meal plans. The most important thing is that you enjoy cooking the food just as much as you do eating them.

## Day 1

Breakfast: Sunny Side Up Eggs over Herbed Mushrooms

Lunch: Arugula, Fig and Prosciutto Salad with Walnut and Parmesan and Oven Roasted Chicken Thighs with Fennel, Orange and Olive Sauce

Snack: Pita Bread and Spanish Chili Garlic Mushrooms

Dinner: Shrimp, Celery, Leek and Fennel Soup

## Day 2

Breakfast: Garlic, Basil and Gruyere Cheese Scramble

Lunch: Greek Sardine and Garden Salad and Oven Roasted Chicken Thighs with Fennel, Orange and Olive Sauce

Snack: Savory Chickpea Flatbread and Goat Cheese and Roasted Bell Pepper Dip

Dinner: Golden Leek and Shellfish Soup

## Day 3

Breakfast: Italian Basil, Tomato and Asparagus Omelette

Lunch: Pear and Arugula Salad with Apricot Vinaigrette, Almonds and Goat Cheese and Spicy Moroccan Lamb and Lentil Stew

Snack: Pita Bread and Spanish Chili Garlic Mushrooms

Dinner: Broiled Mackerel with Lemon and Israeli Green Hot Sauce with Italian Spinach, Parmesan and Brown Rice Soup

## Day 4

Breakfast: Breakfast Burritos of Roasted Red Pepper and Mackerel

Lunch: Spiced Egg and Spinach Salad and Spicy Moroccan Lamb and Lentil Stew

Snack: Savory Chickpea Flatbread and Goat Cheese and Roasted Bell Pepper Dip

Dinner: Braised Halibut with Dijon Mustard Leeks with Moroccan Tomato Soup

## Day 5

Breakfast: Baked Sausage and Vegetable Frittata

Lunch: Red Pepper, Asparagus and Spinach Salad with Goat Cheese and Spanish Style Saffron and Pork Meatball Soup

Snack: Pita Bread and Green Olive and Lentil Dip

Dinner: Grilled Tender Chicken Kebabs with Tomato and Feta Salad


## Day 6

Breakfast: No Crust Greek Style Cheesy Spinach Quiche

Lunch: Hot Cauliflower and Feta Salad with Herbed Dressing and Spanish Style Saffron and Pork Meatball Soup

Snack: Savory Chickpea Flatbread and Goat Cheese and Roasted Bell Pepper Dip

Dinner: Herbed Lemon Haddock Fillets with Garlic Potatoes with Turkish Bulgur, Red Pepper and Tomato Soup


## Day 7

Breakfast: No Crust Cheesy Broccoli and Tarragon Quiche

Lunch: Radicchio, Date, and Citrus Salad with Smoked Almonds and Libyan Lamb and Mint Sharba

Snack: Pita Bread and Green Olive and Lentil Dip

Dinner: Grilled Mackerel with Marjoram and Lemon with Spiced Fava Bean Soup

Mediterranean Diet One Week Menu

# Chapter 3 – Breakfast Recipes

## Sunny Side Up Eggs over Herbed Mushrooms

*Number of Servings: 3*

*Cooking and Preparation Time: 10 minutes*

### Ingredients:

- 6 large eggs
- 1 large red onion, peeled and chopped
- 1 large garlic clove, peeled and minced
- 3 cups sliced large button mushrooms
- ½ cup crumbled feta cheese
- 3 Tbsp. extra virgin olive oil
- 1 ½ tsp. dried thyme
- ¾ tsp. dried oregano
- Sea salt, to taste
- Freshly ground black pepper, to taste

### How to Prepare:

1. Place a non-stick skillet over high flame and add 1 ½ tablespoons of olive oil. Swirl to coat.
2. Saute the onion until translucent, then add the garlic and sauté until fragrant.

15

3.  Stir in the mushrooms with the thyme, oregano, salt, and pepper. Saute until tender.
4.  Divide the mushrooms into three servings then set aside.
5.  Wipe the skillet clean and place over medium flame. Add the remaining olive oil.
6.  Break one egg into the skillet and cook until the white is set and the yolk is cooked to a desired consistency. Transfer to a heap of mushrooms.
7.  Cook the next egg and then place on top of another pile of mushrooms, followed by the third.
8.  Season each serving with some salt and pepper. Then, top with feta. Best served right away.

# Garlic, Basil and Gruyere Cheese Scramble

*Number of Servings: 3*

*Cooking and Preparation Time: 10 minutes*

## Ingredients:

- 6 large eggs
- 3 garlic cloves, peeled and crushed
- 3 Tbsp. chopped fresh basil
- 3 Tbsp. freshly grated Gruyere cheese
- 3 tsp. olive oil

## How to Prepare:

1. Whisk the eggs in a large bowl together with 3 tablespoons of water. Add the basil and cheese and whisk again to combine.
2. Place a large non-stick skillet over low flame and heat through. Once hot, add the olive oil and swirl to coat.
3. Sauté the garlic until golden brown and fragrant. Pour the egg mixture into the skillet then sauté until scrambled and fluffy.
4. Divide the scrambled eggs into three servings. Best served right away.

# Italian Basil, Tomato and Asparagus Omelette

*Number of Servings: 6*

*Cooking and Preparation Time: 20 minutes*

## Ingredients:

- 18 thin fresh asparagus stalks, trimmed
- 3 scallions, white and light green, sliced thinly
- 2 large garlic cloves, peeled and minced
- 2 ripe plum tomatoes, seeded and diced
- 9 large eggs
- ½ cup freshly grated Parmesan cheese
- 1 ½ Tbsp. extra virgin olive oil
- 3 tsp. chopped fresh basil
- Sea salt, to taste
- Freshly ground black pepper, to taste

## How to Prepare:

1. Set the oven to broil and place the oven rack 8 inches away from the heat source.
2. Boil a pan of salted water over high flame, then add the asparagus and blanch for 3 minutes.
3. Drain the asparagus right after then rinse in ice water to stop the cooking process. Drain thoroughly then chop the asparagus into bite-sized pieces.

4. Beat the eggs in a bowl then add a pinch of salt and pepper. Whisk well then add the parmesan cheese and beat to combine.

5. Place a cast iron skillet over high flame and heat through. Then, add the olive oil and swirl to coat.

6. Saute the scallions and garlic until tender. Then, add the asparagus until tender. Stir in the tomatoes and basil and stir well to combine.

7. Add the eggs over the vegetable mixture then tilt to even out in the pan. Then, reduce to low flame and cook the frittata until the bottom is set.

8. Transfer the pan to the oven and broil the frittata for about 3 minutes, or until the top is golden brown.

9. Take the frittata out of the oven and slice it into 8 wedges. Best served warm.

# Breakfast Burritos of Roasted Red Pepper and Mackerel

*Number of Servings: 3*

*Cooking and Preparation Time: 15 minutes*

## Ingredients:

- 6 large eggs
- 12 oz. canned mackerel in brine, drained and flaked
- 1 large white onion, peeled and chopped
- 1 large roasted sweet red pepper, drained and chopped
- 3 large ripe plum tomatoes, seeded and diced
- 3 Tbsp. extra virgin olive oil
- 1 tsp. dried tarragon
- Sea salt, to taste
- Freshly ground black pepper, to taste

## How to Prepare:

1. Place a large non-stick skillet over medium flame and heat through. Once hot, add 1 ½ tablespoons olive oil and swirl to coat.
2. Stir in the onion and sauté until tender. Then, stir in the tomatoes, peppers, flaked mackerel, and tarragon. Saute until heated through.
3. Reduce to low flame and cook for 5 minutes, or until the liquids in the mixture is reduced.
4. Turn off the heat and set the skillet aside to cool the mixture.

5. Whisk the eggs with a pinch of salt and pepper, then stir in the mackerel mixture and mix well.
6. Wipe the skillet clean then place over medium flame. Add the mixture and scramble until cooked through. Turn off the heat and set aside.
7. Heat the tortilla through then divide the scrambled mixture among each. Roll up and serve right away.

# Baked Sausage and Vegetable Frittata

*Number of Servings: 6*

*Cooking and Preparation Time: 30 minutes*

## Ingredients:

- 5 large eggs
- 4 egg whites
- 2 pieces Mediterranean garlic sausages, 6 inches each, diced
- 2 ripe tomatoes, seeded and diced
- 2 garlic cloves, peeled and minced
- 3 Tbsp. chopped fresh flat leaf parsley
- 3 Tbsp. freshly grated Parmesan cheese
- 3 tsp. olive oil

## How to Prepare:

1. Set the oven to 375 degrees F to preheat.
2. Beat the eggs in a large bowl and season lightly with salt and pepper. Set aside.
3. Place a large cast iron skillet over medium flame and add the olive oil. Swirl to coat, then add the sausage and cook until browned all over.
4. Stir in the tomato and garlic and sauté until the liquids are mostly evaporated. Stir in the parsley and season with salt and pepper.
5. Whisk the eggs once more then pour into the skillet and tilt to spread the eggs out evenly.

6. Top the eggs on top of the eggs then transfer the skillet to the preheated oven.
7. Bake the frittata for 12 minutes, or until set.
8. Remove from the oven then slice into six equal wedges. Best served right away.

# No Crust Greek Style Cheesy Spinach Quiche

*Number of Servings: 4*

*Cooking and Preparation Time: 1 hour*

## Ingredients:

- 3 large eggs
- 2 egg whites
- 3 scallions, chopped
- 2 cups steamed spinach
- 1/3 cup light cream
- 1/3 cup grated Greek graviera cheese
- 1 ½ tsp. extra virgin olive oil
- 1/3 tsp. cayenne pepper
- 1/3 tsp. ground nutmeg
- Sea salt, to taste
- Freshly ground black pepper, to taste
- Olive oil cooking spray

## How to Prepare:

1. Set the oven to 350 degrees F to preheat. Lightly coat a pie plate with olive oil cooking spray and set aside.
2. Press as much of the liquids out of the steamed spinach as possible, then chop and set aside.

3. Place a skillet over medium flame and add the olive oil. Swirl to coat then sauté the scallions until tender. Turn off the heat.

4. Beat the eggs and egg whites in a large bowl until smooth. Add the cream and mix well. Then, sprinkle in the nutmeg, cayenne, and salt and pepper to taste. Mix well.

5. Stir the spinach, scallions, and graviera cheese into the egg mixture, then pour into the prepared pie plate.

6. Bake the quiche for 30 minutes, uncovered, until set and golden brown.

7. Transfer to a cooling rack and let set for about 5 minutes. Then, slice into four equal portions. Best served warm.

# No Crust Cheesy Broccoli and Tarragon Quiche

*Number of Servings: 6*

*Cooking and Preparation Time: 1 hour*

## Ingredients:

- 4 scallions, chopped
- 4 large eggs
- 1 ½ cups chopped broccoli florets
- 1/3 cup light cream
- 1/3 cup mild goat cheese
- 1/3 cup freshly grated Gruyere cheese
- 1 ½ tsp. extra virgin olive oil
- ¾ tsp. dried tarragon
- Sea salt, to taste
- Freshly ground black pepper, to taste

## How to Prepare:

1. Preheat the oven to 350 degrees F.
2. Lightly oil the inside of a large pie plate with olive oil.
3. Whisk the eggs together with the cream until smooth. Season to taste with salt and pepper, then add the tarragon and whisk well to combine.
4. Sprinkle the cheeses into the egg mixture and whisk again until combined.

5. Place a large skillet over medium flame and heat through. Add the olive oil and swirl to coat, then add the scallions and sauté until tender.

6. Add the broccoli florets and sauté until tender, then stir into the egg mixture.

7. Whisk the egg and broccoli mixture once again before pouring into the prepared pie plate.

8. Bake the quiche in the preheated oven for 30 minutes, or until set and golden brown. Transfer to a cooling rack and let stand for 5 minutes.

9. Slice the quiche into six equal wedges and serve right away.

# Shakshuka

*Number of Servings: 2*

*Cooking and Preparation Time: 25 minutes*

**Ingredients:**

- 2 large fresh eggs
- 1 large onion, peeled and chopped
- 1 yellow bell pepper, stemmed, cored, seeded, and diced
- 3 garlic cloves, peeled and minced
- 8 oz. canned diced tomatoes
- 1 cup jarred piquillo peppers, chopped
- ¼ cup crumbled feta cheese
- 3 Tbsp. chopped fresh cilantro
- 2 ½ Tbsp. water
- 1 ½ Tbsp. extra virgin olive oil
- 1 tsp. tomato paste
- ¾ tsp. ground turmeric
- ¾ tsp. ground cumin
- 1 bay leaf
- Cayenne pepper, to taste
- Sea salt, to taste
- Freshly ground black pepper, to taste

**How to Prepare:**

1. Place a large skillet over medium-high flame. Once hot, add the olive oil and swirl to coat.
2. Stir in the onion and bell pepper and sauté until tender. Stir in the garlic, tomato paste, cumin, turmeric, and a pinch each of cayenne, salt, and black pepper. Mix everything well.
3. Add the piquillo peppers, water, bay leaf, and tomatoes with their juices. Stir and bring to a simmer.
4. Continue to simmer until the sauce thickens. Then, remove and discard the bay leaf. Add half the cilantro and stir well to combine. Turn off and allow to cool slightly.
5. Once cooled, pour two thirds of the mixture into a food processor or blender and process until smooth. Pour the puree back into the skillet and stir to combine.
6. Reheat the sauce over medium low flame, then create two shallow pits in the sauce. Crack each egg open and slide into one of the pits. Season lightly with salt and pepper.
7. Once both eggs are in the sauce, cover the skillet and cook until set.
8. Top the shakshuka with feta and the remaining cilantro, then serve right away.

# Chapter 4 –Salads

## Arugula, Fig and Prosciutto Salad with Walnut and Parmesan

*Number of Servings: 3*

*Cooking and Preparation Time: 15 minutes*

**Ingredients:**

- 1 small shallot, minced
- 4 cups baby arugula
- 1 oz. thinly sliced prosciutto, sliced into thin ribbons
- 1 oz. shaved Parmesan cheese
- ¼ cup stemmed and chopped dried figs
- ¼ cup toasted and chopped walnuts
- 1 ½ Tbsp. balsamic vinegar
- ½ Tbsp. raspberry jam
- 2 Tbsp. olive oil
- Sea salt, to taste
- Freshly ground black pepper, to taste

**How to Prepare:**

1. In a mixing bowl, whisk together the jam, vinegar, shallot, and a pinch of salt and pepper. Add the figs, then cover and microwave for 1 minute.
2. Whisk the fig mixture well then add the remaining olive oil. Whisk well until the figs are tender. Set aside.
3. Place a skillet over medium flame. Once hot, add ½ tablespoon of olive oil to coat the bottom of the pan.
4. Add the prosciutto and cook until crisp, then transfer to a plate lined with paper towels and set aside.
5. Place the arugula in a salad bowl and add the vinaigrette on top. Toss well to coat then season with salt and pepper.
6. Divide the arugula into individual servings then top with prosciutto, walnuts, and parmesan cheese. Best served right away.

# Greek Sardine and Garden Salad

*Number of Servings: 3*

*Cooking and Preparation Time: 15 minutes*

## Ingredients:

- 1 small cucumber, peeled, quartered and diced
- 2 large tomatoes, seeded and diced
- 1 small red onion, peeled and diced
- 2 sardine fillets in olive oil, drained and chopped
- 2 whole sardine fillets in olive oil
- 1/3 cup chopped arugula leaves
- ¼ cup chopped fresh flat leaf parsley

*For the dressing:*

- 2 ½ Tbsp extra virgin olive oil
- ½ Tbsp. freshly squeezed lemon juice
- Sea salt, to taste
- Freshly ground black pepper, to taste

## How to Prepare:

1. First make the dressing by combining all the dressing ingredients in a mason jar. Seal and shake vigorously to combine.

2. In a large salad bowl, combine the cucumber, tomatoes, red onion, parsley, and arugula. Add the chopped sardine fillets and toss again to combine.
3. Divide the salad into three servings then divide the whole sardine fillets among them.
4. Drizzle the dressing over the salad, give it a light toss, and then serve right away.

# Pear and Arugula Salad with Apricot Vinaigrette, Almonds and Goat Cheese

*Number of Servings: 3*

*Cooking and Preparation Time: 15 minutes*

## Ingredients:

- 1 small shallot, minced
- 1 small ripe pear, halved, cored, and sliced
- 4 cups baby arugula
- 1/3 cup crumbled goat cheese
- ¼ cup chopped dried apricots
- 3 Tbsp. toasted sliced almonds
- 1 ½ Tbsp. white wine vinegar
- 1 ½ Tbsp. extra virgin olive oil
- ½ Tbsp. apricot jam
- Sea salt, to taste
- Freshly ground black pepper, to taste

## How to Prepare:

1. Combine the apricot jam, vinegar, and shallot in a bowl and season with salt and pepper. Whisk well to combine.
2. Add the dried apricots into the mixture and stir well. Then, cover and microwave for 1 minute.

3. Carefully take the vinaigrette out of the microwave and then whisk well. Gradually whisk in the olive oil, then add the onion and stir well.
4. Divide the arugula into individual servings then add the pear. Season lightly with salt and pepper, and then drizzle the apricot vinaigrette on top.
5. Top with almonds and goat cheese then serve right away.

# Spiced Egg and Spinach Salad

*Number of Servings: 3*

*Cooking and Preparation Time: 20 minutes*

## Ingredients:

- 1 ripe tomato, chopped
- 1 small garlic clove, peeled and minced
- 2 small hard-boiled eggs, peeled and quartered
- 6 salt-cured olives
- ¼ lb. spinach, chopped
- 2 ½ Tbsp. extra virgin olive oil
- 1 Tbsp. sherry vinegar
- ¼ tsp. ground cumin
- ¼ tsp. sweet Hungarian paprika
- Cayenne pepper, to taste
- Sea salt, to taste
- Freshly ground black pepper, to taste

## How to Prepare:

1. Place the tomatoes in a bowl and add the garlic, vinegar, and 1 ¼ tablespoons of olive oil.
2. Add the cumin and paprika then toss well to coat. Season to taste with cayenne pepper, salt, and black pepper. Set aside.

3. Place the greens into a salad bowl and add the rest of the olive oil. Then, season with salt and pepper and add the tomato mixture. Toss everything to combine.
4. Divide the salad into individual servings then divide the sliced eggs among them. Best served right away.

# Red Pepper, Asparagus and Spinach Salad with Goat Cheese

*Number of Servings: 3*

*Cooking and Preparation Time: 15 minutes*

## Ingredients:

- 1 small red bell pepper, stemmed, cored, seeded and sliced into thin strips
- 1 shallot, halved and thinly sliced
- 1 garlic clove, peeled and minced
- ½ lb. asparagus, trimmed and sliced on the diagonal
- 3 cups baby spinach
- ¼ cup crumbled goat cheese
- 2 ½ Tbsp. extra virgin olive oil
- ½ Tbsp. and ½ tsp. sherry vinegar
- Sea salt, to taste
- Freshly ground black pepper, to taste

## How to Prepare:

1. Combine the vinegar, garlic, and a pinch of salt and pepper in a bowl. Whisk well then gradually drizzle in the olive oil as you continue to whisk.
2. Place a skillet over high flame and add ½ tablespoon of oil. Swirl to coat, then sauté the bell pepper until pale brown.

3. Add the asparagus and season with salt and pepper. Sauté until the asparagus is bite tender.
4. Add the shallot and mix well with the asparagus. Continue to sauté for about a minute, then transfer to a bowl and set aside.
5. Place the spinach in a bowl and add 1 tablespoon of the vinaigrette. Toss well to coat, then season to taste with salt and pepper.
6. Divide the spinach into individual servings, then add the asparagus on top. Top with goat cheese then serve right away.

# Hot Cauliflower and Feta Salad with Herbed Dressing

*Number of Servings: 4*

*Cooking and Preparation Time: 20 minutes*

## Ingredients:

- 1 garlic clove, peeled and diced
- 1 lb. cauliflower, trimmed and chopped into florets
- 2 ½ Tbsp. extra virgin olive oil
- 2 Tbsp. crumbled feta cheese
- 1 ½ Tbsp. freshly squeezed lemon juice
- 1 Tbsp. toasted pine nuts
- ½ tsp. chopped fresh flat leaf parsley
- ½ tsp. chopped fresh basil
- ½ tsp. chopped fresh mint
- Sea salt, to taste
- Freshly ground black pepper, to taste

## How to Prepare:

1. Combine the olive oil, garlic, basil, parsley, mint, and lemon juice in a bowl and whisk vigorously. Season to taste with salt and pepper then whisk again to combine. Set aside.
2. Simmer a saucepan over salted water over medium-high flame then add the cauliflower florets. Steam for about 6 minutes, or until crisp tender. Drain the cauliflower then transfer to a bowl and set aside.

3. Transfer the cauliflower to a salad bowl and add the dressing. Toss to coat, then sprinkle with feta cheese and pine nuts. Best served right away.

# Radicchio, Date, and Citrus Salad with Smoked Almonds

*Number of Servings: 3*

*Cooking and Preparation Time: 15 minutes*

## Ingredients:

- 3 oz. radicchio, cored and thinly sliced
- 1 red grapefruit, peeled and sliced into segments
- 2 small oranges, peeled and sliced into segments
- 1 small shallot, minced
- 1/3 cup chopped pitted dates
- ¼ cup chopped smoked almonds
- 1 ½ Tbsp. extra virgin olive oil
- ½ tsp. brown sugar
- ½ tsp. Dijon mustard
- Sea salt, to taste
- Freshly ground black pepper, to taste

## How to Prepare:

1. Place the sliced grapefruit and oranges into a large bowl and add the sugar with a pinch of salt. Toss everything to combine then set aside for 15 minutes.
2. After 15 minutes, strain the fruit and save 1 tablespoon of the juice. Place the fruit on a serving dish and drizzle with olive oil.

3. Pour the juice into a bowl and stir in the mustard and shallot. Mix well then add the radicchio, 3 tablespoons of dates, and 2 tablespoons of almonds. Toss everything to combine.
4. Divide the citrus into individual servings, then heap the radicchio salad on top. Add the rest of the dates on top then sprinkle with almonds. Serve immediately.

# Moroccan Chili Tomato Salad

*Number of Servings: 3*

*Cooking and Preparation Time: 15 minutes*

## Ingredients:

- 2 large ripe tomatoes, diced
- 1 small cucumber, peeled, seeded and diced
- 1 large green bell pepper
- 1 red or green chili pepper
- 2 ½ Tbsp. chopped fresh flat leaf parsley
- 1 ½ Tbsp. freshly squeezed lemon juice
- 1 Tbsp. extra virgin olive oil
- ¼ tsp. ground cumin
- Sea salt, to taste
- Freshly ground black pepper, to taste

## How to Prepare:

1. Set the broiler to medium-high to preheat. Once hot, broil the bell pepper and chili pepper until tender and charred.
2. Transfer the peppers into a paper bag, seal, then set aside to cool.
3. Once the peppers are cool to the touch, put on plastic gloves and skin them carefully. Then, chop them and place in a large bowl.
4. Add the tomatoes, parsley, cucumber, olive oil, lemon juice, and cumin to the bowl, mixing well. Season with salt and pepper and toss again to combine.

5. Cover the bowl and let stand for 20 minutes to let the flavors meld before serving. Serve while it is still warm.

# Asparagus, Orange and Hazelnut Pesto Salad with Feta

*Number of Servings: 3*

*Cooking and Preparation Time: x minutes*

**Ingredients:**

- 1 lb. asparagus, trimmed and chopped into bite-sized pieces on the diagonal
- 1 orange, peeled and sliced into segments
- ½ cup crumbled feta cheese
- 1/3 cup chopped toasted hazelnuts
- Sea salt, to taste
- Freshly ground black pepper, to taste

*For the Pesto:*

- 1 small garlic clove, peeled and minced
- 1 cup fresh mint leaves
- ¼ cup extra virgin olive oil
- 2 Tbsp. fresh basil leaves
- 2 Tbsp. grated Pecorino Romano cheese
- 1 tsp. freshly squeezed lemon juice
- ½ tsp. freshly grated lemon zest
- Sea salt, to taste
- Freshly ground black pepper, to taste

**How to Prepare:**

1. First make the pesto by combining the basil, mint, lemon juice and zest, garlic, Pecorino, and 1/3 teaspoon of salt in a food processor. Cover and process until finely chopped.
2. Gradually drizzle the olive oil into the food processor with the herb mixture. Blend until smooth then season with salt and pepper to taste. Set aside.
3. Place the asparagus in a bowl with water and microwave for 1 minute or until bite tender. Place in a mixing bowl.
4. Add the feta, orange segments, and hazelnuts into the bowl of asparagus, and then add the pesto. Toss well to coat and season to taste with salt and pepper. Best served right away.

# Zesty Fennel and Romaine Lettuce Salad

*Number of Servings: 3*

*Cooking and Preparation Time: 20 minutes*

## Ingredients:

- 3 large radishes, halved and sliced
- 1 small navel orange, peeled and diced
- 6 Moroccan olives, pitted
- ½ fennel bulb, trimmed, quartered and sliced thinly
- 2 cups shredded romaine lettuce
- ¼ cup chopped fresh dill
- 2 ½ Tbsp. extra virgin olive oil
- 1 ½ Tbsp. sherry vinegar
- ¼ tsp. crushed fennel seeds
- ¼ tsp. black or rose peppercorns
- Sea salt, to taste
- Freshly ground black pepper, to taste

## How to Prepare:

1. Combine the olive oil, fennel seeds, peppercorns, and vinegar in a small jar and seal tightly.
2. Shake the jar vigorously then season to taste with salt and pepper. Seal and shake again. Set aside to let the flavors meld.

3. In a large salad bowl, toss together the fennel, lettuce, dill, olives, and diced navel orange.

4. Drizzle the dressing over the salad and toss well to coat. Best served right away.

# Brussels Sprouts and Pecorino Salad with Pine Nuts

*Number of Servings: 3*

*Cooking and Preparation Time: 15 minutes*

## Ingredients:

- 1 shallot, minced
- 1 small garlic clove, peeled and minced
- ½ lb. Brussels sprouts, trimmed, halved, and sliced thinly
- 1/3 cup shredded Pecorino Romano cheese
- 2 Tbsp. toasted pine nuts
- 2 Tbsp. extra virgin olive oil
- 1 Tbsp. freshly squeezed lemon juice
- ½ Tbsp. Dijon mustard
- Sea salt, to taste
- Freshly ground black pepper, to taste

## How to Prepare:

1. In a large mixing bowl, whisk together the mustard, lemon juice, garlic, and ¼ teaspoon of salt. Then, gradually drizzle in the olive oil as you continue to whisk the dressing.
2. Place the Brussels sprouts into the dressing and toss well to coat. Cover the bowl and refrigerate for up to 2 hours.
3. After 2 hours, add the Pecorino and pine nuts then toss well. Season to taste with salt and pepper and toss again. Best served right away.

# Green Beans, Onions and Ham Salad

*Number of Servings: 3*

*Cooking and Preparation Time: 15 minutes*

## Ingredients:

- 1 small white onion, peeled and minced
- 1 roasted red bell pepper in brine, drained and diced
- 1 oz. Spanish ham (prosciutto di Parma), chopped
- 1 small hard-boiled egg, peeled and chopped
- ½ lb. green beans, trimmed
- 2 ½ Tbsp. chopped fresh flat leaf parsley
- 1 ½ Tbsp. red wine vinegar
- Sea salt, to taste
- Freshly ground black pepper, to taste

## How to Prepare:

1. First combine the olive oil and red wine vinegar in a bowl and whisk vigorously. Season to taste with salt and pepper then set aside.
2. Fill a small saucepan with salted water and bring to a boil over high flame. Reduce to a simmer then add the green beans.
3. Cook the green beans for 8 minutes, or until crisp tender, then drain and rinse under cold running water to prevent overcooking. Set aside to drain.

4. Place the green beans into a salad bowl and add the minced onion, ham, egg, peppers, and parsley. Drizzle in the dressing then toss everything to coat. Best served right away.

# Peppery Greens and Olive Salad with Feta Cheese

*Number of Servings: 3*

*Cooking and Preparation Time: 15 minutes*

## Ingredients:

- 1 small garlic clove, peeled and minced
- ½ lb. escarole, trimmed and chopped into bite-sized pieces
- 2 oz. trimmed frisee
- ¼ cup halved pitted kalamata olives
- ¼ cup crumbled feta cheese
- 2 ½ Tbsp. pepperoncini, seeded and sliced into strips
- 2 ½ Tbsp. chopped fresh dill
- 1 ½ Tbsp. extra virgin olive oil
- 1 Tbsp. freshly squeezed lemon juice
- Sea salt, to taste
- Freshly ground black pepper, to taste

## How to Prepare:

1. Combine the dill, lemon juice, garlic, and a pinch of salt and pepper in a separate bowl. Whisk vigorously to combine, then gradually whisk in the olive oil. Set aside.
2. Place the escarole, frisee, olives, pepperoncini, and feta in a salad bowl and toss well to combine.
3. Drizzle the dressing over the salad and toss well to coat, then divide into individual servings. Best served right away.

# Classic Caponata

*Number of Servings: 2*

*Cooking and Preparation Time: 30 minutes preparation time*

## Ingredients:

- 1 garlic clove, peeled and minced
- 1 large ripe tomato, peeled, seeded and cubed
- ¾ lb. eggplant, sliced into bite-sized cubes
- 1 small red onion, peeled and chopped
- 1 ½ Tbsp. extra virgin olive oil
- 1 Tbsp. chopped fresh oregano
- 1 Tbsp. chopped fresh flat leaf parsley
- ½ Tbsp. capers
- Freshly ground black pepper, to taste
- Sea salt, to taste

## How to Prepare:

1. Place the cubed eggplant into a colander and sprinkle with salt. Toss to combine, then place a plate on top of the eggplant.
2. Add a weight such as a can of beans on top of the plate to press down on the eggplant and drain the excess liquids. Set aside for 1 hour.
3. After the eggplants have been drained, blot them dry with paper towels and set aside.

4. Place a non-stick skillet over high flame and heat through. Add ¾ tablespoon of olive oil and swirl to coat, then add the eggplant cubes and stir until browned. Transfer to a bowl and set aside.

5. Return the pan to the heat and reduce to low flame. Add the remaining olive oil and swirl to coat then stir in the onions. Sauté until golden, then stir in the garlic and sauté until fragrant.

6. Add the tomatoes and sauté until tender, then add the eggplant back to the pan and stir to combine and heat through.

7. Add the capers and oregano to the pan and mix well. Season to taste with salt and pepper.

8. Continue to simmer until all the ingredients are tender. Remove from heat and transfer to a serving bowl. Allow to cool for 5 minutes before serving. Best served warm.

# Classic Nicoise Salad

*Number of Servings: 3*

*Cooking and Preparation Time: x minutes*

**Ingredients:**

- 2 small hard-boiled eggs, peeled and quartered
- 1 lb. Bibb or Boston lettuce, torn
- ¾ lb. small red potatoes, scrubbed clean and quartered
- 4 oz. green beans, trimmed and halved
- 2 ½ oz. canned solid white tuna in water, drained and flaked
- 2 small tomatoes, cored and sliced into wedges
- 1 small red onion, peeled and sliced thinly
- 2 Tbsp. pitted nicoise olives
- 1 Tbsp. dry vermouth
- Sea salt, to taste
- Freshly ground black pepper, to taste

*For the Dressing*

- 1 small shallot, minced
- ¼ cup extra virgin olive oil
- 2 Tbsp. freshly squeezed lemon juice
- 1 Tbsp. minced fresh basil
- 1 tsp. minced fresh oregano
- 1 tsp. minced fresh thyme
- ½ tsp. Dijon mustard
- ¼ tsp. sea salt

- Freshly ground black pepper, to taste

## How to Prepare:

1. First make the dressing by combining the lemon juice, basil, oregano, thyme, shallot, mustard, and a pinch of salt and pepper in a bowl. Whisk well, then gradually mix in the olive oil. Set aside.
2. Place the potatoes in a saucepan and add enough water to cover. Cover the pan and place over high flame, then bring to a boil. Once boiling, stir in ½ tablespoon of salt and let simmer.
3. Cook the potatoes until tender, then remove with a slotted spoon and transfer to a bowl.
4. Add 2 tablespoons of vinaigrette to the potatoes along with the vermouth. Toss well to coat, then season to taste with salt and pepper and set aside.
5. Place the lettuce in a bowl and add 2 tablespoons of vinaigrette. Toss well to coat, then arrange on a serving dish.
6. Place the tuna in the bowl in which the lettuce was prepared, then add 2 tablespoons of vinaigrette. Toss well to combine, then heap on top of the lettuce.
7. Place the tomatoes and red onion in the same bowl, then add 1 tablespoon of vinaigrette. Season with salt and pepper then toss well to coat.
8. Place the tomato wedges on the salad together with the potatoes.
9. Bring the same water in which the potatoes were prepared to a boil. Stir in ½ tablespoon of salt then add the green beans. Cook until crisp tender.
10. Drain the green beans then place in the ice water to stop the cooking process.

11. Drain the green beans well and blot dry with paper towels. Place in the salad bowl and add 1 tablespoon of vinaigrette. Season with salt and pepper then toss to coat.
12. Arrange the green beans on the salad, followed by the eggs and olives. Serve right away.

# Chapter 5 – Light Soups

## Sicilian Escarole and Chickpea Soup

*Number of Servings: 4*

*Cooking and Preparation Time: 1 hour*

**Ingredients:**

- 1 small onion, peeled and chopped
- 3 small garlic cloves, peeled and minced
- 1 small tomato, chopped
- 1 fennel bulb, trimmed, halved, cored, and chopped
- ½ lb. escarole, trimmed and chopped
- 1 ½ inches orange zest strip
- ½ lb. dried chickpeas, rinsed well
- 2 ½ cups vegetable broth
- 1 Tbsp. extra virgin olive oil
- 2 tsp. freshly grated Parmesan cheese
- 1 tsp. minced fresh oregano
- 1 bay leaf
- Red pepper flakes, to taste
- Sea salt, to taste
- Freshly ground black pepper, to taste

## How to Prepare:

1. In a large bowl, stir together 2 quarts of cold water and 1 ½ tablespoons of sea salt. Mix well then add the chickpeas. Cover and soak at room temperature overnight.
2. The following morning, drain the chickpeas and rinse thoroughly. Set aside.
3. Place a stock pot over medium flame and heat through. Once hot, add the olive oil and swirl to coat. Sauté the onion, fennel, and ½ teaspoon of sea salt. Sauté until tender.
4. Add the garlic, oregano, and a pinch of red pepper flakes. Sauté until fragrant.
5. Add 3 ½ cups of water together with the chickpeas, followed by the broth, bay leaf, and orange zest.
6. Increase heat and bring to a boil, then reduce to a simmer. Cook until the chickpeas are tender, about 45 minutes.
7. Add the escarole and tomato and stir until the escarole is wilted. Then, remove and discard the bay leaves. Season to taste with salt and pepper.
8. Ladle into individual bowls and top with parmesan cheese. Best served right away.

# Italian Spinach, Parmesan and Brown Rice Soup

*Number of Servings: 4*

*Cooking and Preparation Time: 20 minutes*

## Ingredients:

- 1 ½ lb. fresh spinach, trimmed and chopped
- 1 small white onion, peeled and chopped
- 1 garlic clove, peeled and chopped
- 4 cups chicken, beef or vegetable broth
- ¼ cup uncooked brown rice
- ½ Tbsp. extra virgin olive oil
- 4 tsp. freshly grated Parmesan cheese
- Sea salt, to taste
- Freshly ground black pepper, to taste

## How to Prepare:

1. Place a soup pot over medium flame and heat through. Once hot, add the olive oil and swirl to coat.
2. Saute the onion until translucent, then add the garlic and sauté until fragrant.
3. Stir in the spinach and cook until wilted. Then, transfer everything into a bowl. Do not drain the liquids from the pot.
4. Add the broth to the pot and stir well to combine. Increase to medium-high flame and bring to a boil.

5. Once boiling, stir in the brown rice and cover. Reduce to low flame and cook for about 15 minutes, or until the rice is tender.
6. Meanwhile, blend the spinach in the food processor until smooth. Then, stir the spinach mixture into the soup, then season to taste with salt and pepper.
7. Ladle into individual bowls and sprinkle with Parmesan cheese. Best served right away.

# Moroccan Tomato Soup

*Number of Servings: 3*

*Cooking and Preparation Time: 25 minutes*

## Ingredients:

- 1 small yellow onion, peeled and chopped
- 4 large ripe tomatoes, chopped
- ½ cinnamon stick
- 1 cup chicken broth
- 1 ½ Tbsp. chopped fresh flat leaf parsley
- 1 Tbsp. chopped fresh cilantro
- 1 Tbsp. extra virgin olive oil
- ½ Tbsp. freshly squeezed lemon juice
- ½ tsp. paprika
- ½ tsp. diced fresh ginger
- ½ tsp. ground cumin
- ½ tsp. honey

## How to Prepare:

1. Place the chopped tomatoes into a food processor and blend until smooth. Set aside.
2. Place a soup pot over medium flame and heat through. Once hot, add the olive oil and swirl to coat.

3. Add the onion and sauté until fragrant then add the ginger, paprika, cumin, and cinnamon. Stir well until fragrant.
4. Add the tomatoes to the pot, followed by the broth, honey, and half each of the cilantro and parsley. Stir well to combine.
5. Increase to medium-high flame and bring to a boil. Once boiling, reduce to a simmer and loosely cover.
6. Cook for 15 minutes, or until the soup is thickened. Then, turn off the heat and allow the soup to cool slightly.
7. Transfer the soup to a container and cover. Refrigerate for 3 hours to chill. Before serving, stir in the lemon juice and remaining cilantro and parsley. Ladle into individual bowls and serve. Best served chilled.

# Spiced Fava Bean Soup

*Number of Servings: 4*

*Cooking and Preparation Time: 1 hour and 30 minutes*

## Ingredients:

- 1 small onion, peeled and chopped
- 3 small garlic cloves, peeled and minced
- 3 cups vegetable broth
- 1 ½ cups dried split fava beans, rinsed thoroughly
- 1 cup water
- 2 Tbsp. freshly squeezed lemon juice
- 1 ½ Tbsp. extra virgin olive oil
- 1 tsp. paprika
- 1 tsp. cumin
- Sea salt, to taste
- Freshly ground black pepper, to taste

## How to Prepare:

1. Place a stock pot over medium flame and heat through. Once hot, add the olive oil and swirl to coat.
2. Sauté the onion with a pinch of salt and pepper and sauté until browned.
3. Add the garlic, cumin, and paprika and sauté until fragrant.
4. Add the beans, water, and broth and then bring to a boil. Once boiling, reduce to a simmer, then cover and cook for 1 hour.

5. After 1 hour, blend the soup until smooth then reheat over low flame. Season to taste with salt and pepper, then stir in the lemon juice.
6. Ladle into individual bowls and serve. Best served right away.

# Turkish Bulgur, Red Pepper and Tomato Soup

*Number of Servings: 4*

*Cooking and Preparation Time: 30 minutes*

## Ingredients:

- 1 small onion, peeled and chopped
- 2 garlic cloves, peeled and minced
- 1 red bell pepper, stemmed, seeded and chopped
- 14 oz. vegetable broth
- 1 cup water
- 1/3 cup rinsed medium grind bulgur
- ¼ cup dry white wine
- 2 ½ Tbsp. chopped fresh mint
- 1 Tbsp. extra virgin olive oil
- ½ tsp. crumbled dried mint
- ¼ tsp. smoked paprika
- Red pepper flakes, to taste
- Sea salt, to taste
- Freshly ground black pepper, to taste

## How to Prepare:

1. Place a stock pot over medium-high flame and heat through. Once hot, add the olive oil and swirl to coat.

2. Stir in the bell pepper, onion, and a pinch of salt and pepper. Sauté until tender then add the garlic, smoked paprika, dried mint, and a pinch of red pepper flakes. Sauté until fragrant.
3. Add the tomato paste and mix well. Stir well to combine, then add the wine and scrape the browned bits off the bottom of the pan.
4. Add the tomatoes and their juices then stir well to combine. Add the broth, bulgur, and water then bring to a simmer.
5. Once simmering, reduce to low flame, cover, and simmer until the bulgur is tender. Season to taste with salt and pepper.
6. Ladle into individual bowls and sprinkle with fresh mint. Best served right away.

# Chapter 6 – Seafood Main Dishes

## Provence Style Fish Soup

*Number of Servings: 4*

*Cooking and Preparation Time: 30 minutes*

**Ingredients:**

- 1 small onion, peeled and chopped
- 1 celery rib, halved and diced
- 1 small fennel bulb, trimmed, halved, cored and diced
- 1 lb. skinless hake fillets, sliced
- 8 oz. bottled clam juice
- 3 oz. chopped pancetta
- 2 cups water
- ½ cup dry white wine
- 1 Tbsp. minced fresh flat leaf parsley
- 1 Tbsp. minced fennel fronds
- ½ Tbsp. extra virgin olive oil
- ½ Tbsp. freshly grated orange zest
- ½ tsp. paprika
- Saffron threads, crumbled
- 1 bay leaf
- Red pepper flakes, to taste
- Sea salt, to taste

- Freshly ground black pepper, to taste

## How to Prepare:

1. Place a stock pot over medium flame and heat through. Once hot, add the olive oil and swirl to coat.
2. Add the pancetta in the pot pot and cook, stirring, until browned all over. Add the celery, fennel, onion, and a pinch of salt. Sauté until browned.
3. Add the garlic with a pinch of saffron threads, pepper flakes, and paprika then sauté until fragrant.
4. Add the wine and scrape off the browned bits stuck to the bottom of the pot. Pour in the water then stir in the clam juice and bay leaf.
5. Increase heat and bring to a boil, then reduce to a simmer and cook for 15 minutes.
6. After 15 minutes, discard the bay leaf and add the hake. Cover and cook for about 8 minutes or until the fish fillets are cooked through.
7. Stir in the fennel fronds, parsley, and orange zest. Simmer for 3 minutes, then season to taste with salt and pepper.
8. Divide the soup into individual portions then serve right away.

Ladle into individual bowls and serve. Best served right away.

# Shrimp, Celery, Leek and Fennel Soup

*Number of Servings: 3*

*Cooking and Preparation Time: 20 minutes*

## Ingredients:

- 1 small leek, whites and tender greens, chopped
- 1 small fennel bulb, trimmed and chopped
- 1 small garlic clove, peeled and crushed
- ¼ lb. medium shrimp, peeled and deveined
- 2 cups vegetable broth
- ½ cup chopped celery
- 3 Tbsp. heavy cream
- 1 Tbsp. extra virgin olive oil
- ½ Tbsp. ouzo
- ½ tsp. freshly squeezed lemon juice
- Sea salt, to taste
- Freshly ground black pepper, to taste

## How to Prepare:

1. Place a soup pot over medium flame and heat through. Once hot, add half the olive oil and swirl to coat.
2. Stir in the chopped fennel, leek, and celery, then sauté until tender. Season to taste with salt and pepper, then stir in the broth.

3. Increase the heat and bring to a boil, then reduce to low flame. Cover and simmer for 15 minutes, or until the vegetables are tender.
4. Remove the pot from the heat and allow to cool slightly. Scoop out most of the vegetables and place in a food processor. Then, process until smooth.
5. Stir the pureed vegetables back into the pot and stir well to combine. Reheat over low flame.
6. While the soup is reheating, place a skillet over medium flame and heat through. Once hot, add the remaining olive oil and swirl to coat. Stir in the garlic.
7. Season the shrimp with salt and pepper, then add the shrimp to the hot skillet and cook until bright pink on both sides.
8. Pour the ouzo over the shrimp and cook until evaporated.
9. Transfer the shrimp and their juices into the soup and stir to combine. Add the cream and stir again until heated through.
10. Sprinkle in the lemon juice and then adjust the seasonings to taste. Ladle into individual bowls and serve. Best served right away.

# Golden Leek and Shellfish Soup

*Number of Servings: 4*

*Cooking and Preparation Time: 30 minutes*

## Ingredients:

- 1 large garlic clove, peeled and minced
- ¾ lb. leeks, white and light green parts
- 8 oz. bottled clam juice
- 6 oz. squid, cleaned and sliced
- 6 oz. large sea scallops, tendons removed
- 4 oz. large shrimp, peeled and deveined, shells saved
- 2 oz, pancetta, diced
- 2 cups water
- ½ cup dry white wine
- 3 Tbsp. minced fresh flat leaf parsley
- 1 ½ Tbsp. tomato paste
- 1 Tbsp. extra virgin olive oil
- ½ tsp. ground coriander
- ½ tsp. freshly grated ginger
- ¼ tsp. ground turmeric
- Red pepper flakes, to taste
- Sea salt, to taste
- Freshly ground black pepper, to taste

**How to Prepare:**

1. Place a stock pot over medium flame and heat through. Once hot, add ½ tablespoon of olive oil and swirl to coat.
2. Stir in the shrimp shells and sauté for about 3 minutes or until browned. Then, pour in the wine and let simmer.
3. Simmer for 2 minutes, then add the water and simmer for 5 minutes. After 5 minutes, strain the stock and discard the solids. Store the stock in a bowl and set aside.
4. Place the stock pot back over medium flame and heat through. Once hot, add the remaining olive oil and swirl to coat.
5. Saute the leeks and pancetta until browned, then add the tomato paste, garlic, ginger, coriander, turmeric, and a pinch of red pepper flakes and sea salt.
6. Add the stock and clam juice, then stir to combine. Scrape the browned bits stuck on the bottom of the pot.
7. Simmer the soup for about 15 minutes, then add the sea scallops and squid and simmer for 2 minutes.
8. Add the shrimp and simmer until cooked through, then cover and simmer for 2 minutes, or until tender.
9. Add the parsley and season to taste with salt and pepper. Ladle into individual bowls and serve. Best served right away.

# Broiled Mackerel with Lemon and Israeli Green Hot Sauce

*Number of Servings: 2*

*Cooking and Preparation Time: 45 minutes*

## Ingredients:

- 2 mackerel fillets, 6 oz. each
- 1 small garlic clove, peeled and minced
- 2 Tbsp. mayonnaise
- ½ Tbsp. minced preserved lemon
- 1/8 tsp. brown sugar
- 1 lemon, sliced into wedges
- Sea salt, to taste
- Freshly ground black pepper, to taste
- Olive oil cooking spray

*For the Israeli Green Hot Sauce:*

- 1 garlic clove, peeled and minced
- 1 green Thai chili pepper, stemmed and chopped
- 1/3 cup fresh cilantro leaves
- ¼ cup fresh flat leaf parsley leaves
- 3 Tbsp. extra virgin olive oil
- ¼ tsp. ground coriander
- 1/8 tsp. ground cardamom
- 1/8 tsp. ground cumin
- Sea salt, to taste

- Ground cloves, to taste

## How to Prepare:

1. First prepare the hot sauce by microwaving the olive oil, cumin, cardamom, coriander, and a pinch of salt and pepper. Then, set aside and let cool slightly.
2. Transfer the mixture into a food processor and add the parsley, cilantro, garlic, and chili pepper. Blend into a paste and transfer to a bowl. Cover and refrigerate for up to 4 days.
3. In a bowl, mix together the mayonnaise, brown sugar, garlic, and preserved lemon. Set aside.
4. Set the oven to broil to preheat. Lightly coat a baking sheet with olive oil cooking spray and set aside.
5. Rinse the mackerel then blot dry with paper towels. Season all over with salt and pepper, then place on the prepared rimmed baking sheet.
6. Spread the mixture on the mackerel fillets then broil for 5 minutes, or until the internal temperature reaches 140 degrees F.
7. Lay the fish fillets on a serving dish and garnish with lemon wedges. Serve with the Israeli green hot sauce on the side.

# Braised Halibut with Dijon Mustard Leeks

*Number of Servings: 3*

*Cooking and Preparation Time: 25 minutes*

## Ingredients:

- 3 skinless halibut fillets, 6 oz. each
- 1 lb. leeks, white and light green parts, halved, thinly sliced, and rinsed thoroughly
- ½ cup dry white wine
- ¾ Tbsp. minced fresh parsley
- ¾ tsp. Dijon mustard
- 1 lemon, sliced into wedges
- Sea salt, to taste
- Freshly ground black pepper, to taste

## How to Prepare:

1. Blot the halibut fillets dry with paper towels then season lightly with salt. Set aside.
2. Place a large skillet over medium-high flame and heat through. Once hot, add the olive oil and swirl to coat.
3. Add the halibut fillets to the hot skillet, skinned side facing up, and cook until opaque for about 4 minutes.
4. Once cooked, transfer the fillets, raw side faced down, on a dish.
5. In the same skillet, sauté the leeks with the mustard until tender. Season with salt then add the wine and bring to a simmer.

6. Place the halibut fillets, raw side facing down, on top of the leeks. Reduce to medium low flame and then cover. Cook until the halibut fillets are flaky and have an internal temperature of 140 degrees F.
7. Remove the halibut fillets from the pan and place on a plate. Cover to keep warm and set aside.
8. Continue to cook the leeks until the liquids slightly thicken. Season with salt and pepper.
9. Plate the halibut fillets in individual servings then heap the leeks to the side. Top with parsley and garnish with lemon wedges. Best served right away.

# Herbed Lemon Haddock Fillets with Garlic Potatoes

*Number of Servings: 2*

*Cooking and Preparation Time: 25 minutes*

## Ingredients:

- 2 halibut fillets, 6 oz. each
- 1 small lemon, sliced into thin rounds
- 2 garlic cloves, peeled and minced
- 2 sprigs fresh thyme
- ¾ lb. russet potatoes, sliced into rounds
- 2 Tbsp. extra virgin olive oil
- Sea salt, to taste
- Freshly ground black pepper, to taste

## How to Prepare:

1. Rinse the fish fillets then blot dry with paper towels. Season all over with salt and pepper then set aside.
2. Set the oven to 425 degrees F to preheat.
3. Place the potato rounds in a bowl and add garlic and 1 tablespoon of olive oil. Season with salt and pepper then toss well to coat.
4. Microwave the potatoes, uncovered, for 12 minutes or until the potatoes are tender.

5. Transfer the potatoes to a baking dish and then place the fillets on top of the potato rounds. Drizzle with the remaining olive oil and lay the thyme sprigs and lemon slices on top.

6. Bake the halibut fillets for 17 minutes, or until the internal temperature is 140 degrees F.

7. Divide the potatoes and fish fillets into individual servings and serve right away.

# Saffron Hake Soup with Potatoes and Chorizo

*Number of Servings: 3*

*Cooking and Preparation Time: 30 minutes*

## Ingredients:

- 1 small onion, peeled and minced
- 3 garlic cloves, peeled and minced
- 3 skinless hake fillets, 6 oz. each
- 6 oz. bottled clam juice
- 3 oz. small red potatoes, scrubbed clean and sliced into thin rounds
- 2 oz. Spanish style chorizo, sliced into thin rounds
- ½ cup water
- 1/3 cup dry white wine
- 1 ½ Tbsp. minced fresh flat leaf parsley
- ¾ Tbsp. extra virgin olive oil
- 1 tsp. freshly squeezed lemon juice
- ¼ tsp. crumbled saffron threads
- 1 bay leaf
- Sea salt, to taste
- Freshly ground black pepper, to taste

## How to Prepare:

1. Place a skillet over medium flame and heat through. Once hot, add the olive oil and swirl to coat.

2. Stir in the chorizo and onion and sauté until the onion is slightly caramelized.

3. Add the garlic and crumbled saffron threads and sauté until fragrant, then add the clam juice, wine, water, bay leaf, and potatoes. Increase heat to bring to a simmer.

4. Once simmering, reduce to medium low flame and cover. Cook for 10 minutes or until the potatoes are fork tender.

5. Meanwhile, rinse the hake fillets then blot dry with paper towels. Season all over with salt and pepper.

6. After the potatoes are cooked, add the hake fillets carefully into the pot with the soup. Cover and simmer for 10 minutes, or until the internal temperature of the hake fillets reach 140 degrees F.

7. Remove and discard they bay leaf. Sprinkle in the lemon juice and season to taste with salt and pepper.

8. Divide the fish and soup into individual servings and top with parsley. Best served right away.

# Braised Cod with Coriander and Carrots

*Number of Servings: 3*

*Cooking and Preparation Time: 25 minutes*

## Ingredients:

- 3 skinless cod fillets, 6 oz. each
- 1 lb. carrots, peeled and shaved into thin ribbons
- 3 shallots, halved and thinly sliced
- ½ cup dry white wine
- ¾ Tbsp. minced fresh cilantro
- 1 tsp. freshly squeezed lemon juice
- ¾ tsp. ground coriander
- Sea salt, to taste
- Freshly ground black pepper, to taste

## How to Prepare:

1. Blot the cod fillets dry with paper towels then season lightly with salt. Set aside.
2. Place a large skillet over medium-high flame and heat through. Once hot, add the olive oil and swirl to coat.
3. Add the cod fillets to the hot skillet, skinned side facing up, and cook until opaque for about 4 minutes.
4. Once cooked, transfer the fillets, raw side faced down, on a dish.

5. In the same skillet, sauté the carrots with the shallots and ground coriander until tender. Season with salt then add the wine and bring to a simmer.

6. Place the cod fillets, raw side facing down, on top of the carrots. Reduce to medium low flame and then cover. Cook until the cod fillets are flaky and have an internal temperature of 140 degrees F.

7. Remove the cod fillets from the pan and place on a plate. Cover to keep warm and set aside.

8. Continue to cook the carrots until the liquids slightly thicken. Stir in the lemon juice then season with salt and pepper.

9. Plate the cod fillets in individual servings then heap the carrots to the side. Top with cilantro and garnish with lemon wedges. Best served right away.

# Pan Roasted Striped Cod with Chermoula Sauce

*Number of Servings: 4*

*Cooking and Preparation Time: 25 minutes*

## Ingredients:

- 2 skin on striped cod fillets
- 2 Tbsp. extra virgin olive oil
- Sea salt, to taste
- Freshly ground black pepper, to taste

*For the Chermoula Sauce:*

- 3 garlic cloves, peeled and minced
- ½ cup fresh cilantro leaves
- 1/3 cup extra virgin olive oil
- 1 ½ Tbsp. freshly squeezed lemon juice
- 1/3 tsp. ground cumin
- 1/3 tsp. paprika
- Sea salt, to taste
- Cayenne pepper, to taste

## How to Prepare:

1. Combine the ingredients for the chermoula sauce in a food processor and blend until smooth. Set aside.

2. Set the oven to 325 degrees F to preheat. Place the oven rack in the center section.
3. Blot the cod fillets dry with paper towels then season all over with salt and pepper.
4. Place an ovensafe skillet over medium-high flame and heat through. Once hot, add the olive oil and swirl to coat. Allow to smoke slightly.
5. Add the cod fillets to the hot skillet and brown on one side for about 5 minutes. Flip over then transfer the skillet to the oven.
6. Roast the cod fillets for about 8 minutes or until flaky with an internal temperature of 140 degrees F.
7. Transfer the cod fillets to a chopping board and remove the skins. Divide into individual servings and spoon the chermoula sauce on top. Best served right away.

# Braised Cod with Tarragon Fennel

*Number of Servings: 3*

*Cooking and Preparation Time: 25 minutes*

## Ingredients:

- 3 skinless halibut fillets, 6 oz. each
- 10 oz. fennel bulbs, trimmed, halved, cored, and thinly sliced
- 3 shallots, halved and thinly sliced
- ½ cup dry white wine
- ¾ Tbsp. minced fresh tarragon
- 1 tsp. freshly squeezed lemon juice
- Sea salt, to taste
- Freshly ground black pepper, to taste

## How to Prepare:

1. Blot the cod fillets dry with paper towels then season lightly with salt. Set aside.
2. Place a large skillet over medium-high flame and heat through. Once hot, add the olive oil and swirl to coat.
3. Add the cod fillets to the hot skillet, skinned side facing up, and cook until opaque for about 4 minutes.
4. Once cooked, transfer the fillets, raw side faced down, on a dish.

5. In the same skillet, sauté the fennel with the shallots until tender. Season with salt then add the wine and bring to a simmer.
6. Place the cod fillets, raw side facing down, on top of the fennel. Reduce to medium low flame and then cover. Cook until the cod fillets are flaky and have an internal temperature of 140 degrees F.
7. Remove the cod fillets from the pan and place on a plate. Cover to keep warm and set aside.
8. Continue to cook the fennel until the liquids slightly thicken. Stir in the lemon juice then season with salt and pepper.
9. Plate the cod fillets in individual servings then heap the fennel to the side. Top with tarragon and garnish with lemon wedges. Best served right away.

# Grilled Mackerel with Marjoram and Lemon

*Number of Servings: 3*

*Cooking and Preparation Time: 30 minutes*

## Ingredients:

- 3 whole mackerel, 10 oz. each, gutted and trimmed
- 1 ½ Tbsp. mayonnaise
- 1 ½ tsp. chopped fresh marjoram
- ¾ tsp. freshly grated lemon zest
- 1/3 tsp. raw honey
- 1 lemon, sliced into wedges
- Sea salt, to taste
- Freshly ground black pepper, to taste
- Non-stick cooking spray

## How to Prepare:

1. Rinse the mackerel under cold running water then blot dry with paper towels. Set aside.
2. Sprinkle the lemon zest, marjoram, and a pinch of salt on a chopping board and chop well. Mix well.
3. Open up the cavity of each whole mackerel then season the inside with pepper. Sprinkle the marjoram mixture inside the cavity, then set aside for about 15 minutes.
4. In the meantime, mix together the honey and mayonnaise.

5. After 15 minutes, season the outside of the mackerel with pepper then brush with the honey and mayonnaise mixture.

6. Set the grill to high to preheat. Lightly oil the grate with non-stick cooking spray.

7. Grill the whole mackerels for about 4 minutes per side, or until browned and blistered, with an internal temperature of 135 degrees F.

8. Transfer the whole mackerel to a serving dish and let stand for 5 minutes before serving. Add the lemon wedges then serve right away.

# Grilled Herring with Fennel and Orange

*Number of Servings: 3*

*Cooking and Preparation Time: 30 minutes*

## Ingredients:

- 3 whole herring, 10 oz. each, gutted and trimmed
- 1 ½ Tbsp. mayonnaise
- 1 ½ tsp. ground fennel seeds
- ¾ tsp. freshly grated orange zest
- 1/3 tsp. raw honey
- 1 lemon, sliced into wedges
- Sea salt, to taste
- Freshly ground black pepper, to taste
- Non-stick cooking spray

## How to Prepare:

1. Rinse the herring under cold running water then blot dry with paper towels. Set aside.
2. Sprinkle the orange zest, fennel seeds, and a pinch of salt on a chopping board and chop well. Mix well.
3. Open up the cavity of each whole herring then season the inside with pepper. Sprinkle the fennel seed mixture inside the cavity, then set aside for about 15 minutes.
4. In the meantime, mix together the honey and mayonnaise.

5. After 15 minutes, season the outside of the herring with pepper then brush with the honey and mayonnaise mixture.

6. Set the grill to high to preheat. Lightly oil the grate with non-stick cooking spray.

7. Grill the whole herring for about 4 minutes per side, or until browned and blistered, with an internal temperature of 135 degrees F.

8. Transfer the whole herring to a serving dish and let stand for 5 minutes before serving. Add the lemon wedges then serve right away.

# Grilled Mackerel with Lime and Coriander

*Number of Servings: 3*

*Cooking and Preparation Time: 30 minutes*

## Ingredients:

- 3 whole mackerel, 10 oz. each, gutted and trimmed
- 1 ½ Tbsp. mayonnaise
- 1 ½ tsp. ground coriander
- ¾ tsp. freshly grated lime zest
- 1/3 tsp. raw honey
- 1 lime, sliced into wedges
- Sea salt, to taste
- Freshly ground black pepper, to taste
- Non-stick cooking spray

## How to Prepare:

1. Rinse the mackerel under cold running water then blot dry with paper towels. Set aside.
2. Sprinkle the lime zest, ground coriander, and a pinch of salt on a chopping board and chop well. Mix well.
3. Open up the cavity of each whole mackerel then season the inside with pepper. Sprinkle the coriander mixture inside the cavity, then set aside for about 15 minutes.
4. In the meantime, mix together the honey and mayonnaise.

5. After 15 minutes, season the outside of the mackerel with pepper then brush with the honey and mayonnaise mixture.
6. Set the grill to high to preheat. Lightly oil the grate with non-stick cooking spray.
7. Grill the whole mackerels for about 4 minutes per side, or until browned and blistered, with an internal temperature of 135 degrees F.
8. Transfer the whole mackerel to a serving dish and let stand for 5 minutes before serving. Add the lime wedges then serve right away.

# Chapter 7 – Meat Main Dishes

## Spanish Style Saffron and Pork Meatball Soup

*Number of Servings: 4*

*Cooking and Preparation Time: 45 minutes*

**Ingredients:**

- 1 small onion, peeled and diced
- 1 small red bell pepper, stemmed, cored, seeded and diced
- 1 garlic clove, peeled and minced
- 4 cups chicken broth
- ½ cup dry white wine
- 1 Tbsp. minced fresh flat leaf parsley
- ½ Tbsp. extra virgin olive oil
- ½ tsp. paprika
- Crumbled saffron threads, to taste
- Red pepper flakes, to taste
- Sea salt, to taste
- Freshly ground black pepper, to taste

*For the meatballs:*

- 1 shallot, minced
- 4 oz. lean ground pork
- 4 oz. ground pork

- 1 slice white bread, torn
- ½ cup grated Manchego cheese
- 2 ½ Tbsp. whole milk
- 1 ½ Tbsp. minced fresh flat leaf parsley
- 1 Tbsp. extra virgin olive oil
- ¼ tsp. sea salt
- ¼ tsp. freshly ground black pepper

## How to Prepare:

1. First prepare the meatballs. Combine the bread and milk in a bowl and mash well to combine.
2. Add the remaining ingredients for the meatballs into the bread and milk mixture, then knead to combine.
3. Divide the mixture into 1 inch sized meatballs and arrange on a baking sheet. Cover the baking sheet with plastic wrap and refrigerate for half an hour to firm up.
4. Meanwhile, place a stock pot over medium-high flame and heat through. Once hot, add the olive oil and swirl to coat.
5. Sauté the bell pepper and onion until tender, then stir in the garlic, saffron, paprika, and red pepper flakes. Stir well until fragrant.
6. Add the wine and then scrape up the browned bits from the bottom of the pan. Add the broth and bring to a simmer. Once simmering, add the meatballs and cook for 15 minutes, or until the meatballs are cooked through.
7. Season to taste with salt and pepper and then stir in the parsley. Ladle into soup bowls and serve right away.

# Grilled Tender Chicken Kebabs with Tomato and Feta Salad

*Number of Servings: 4*

*Cooking and Preparation Time: 30 minutes*

## Ingredients:

- 1 lb. boneless, skinless chicken breasts, sliced into 1 inch cubes
- 2 garlic cloves, peeled and minced
- 1 red onion, peeled and sliced thinly
- ¾ cup crumbled feta cheese
- 4 Tbsp. plain Greek yogurt
- 3 Tbsp. extra virgin olive oil
- 2 Tbsp. freshly squeezed lemon juice
- ¾ Tbsp. minced fresh oregano
- ¾ tsp. freshly grated lemon zest
- Sea salt, to taste
- Freshly ground black pepper, to taste

## How to Prepare:

1. Preheat the grill to medium-high.
2. Mix together the lemon juice and zest with the olive oil, garlic, and oregano. Whisk vigorously then season with salt and pepper to taste.

3.  Pour half the mixture into a large nonreactive bowl and stir in the tomatoes and onion. Fold in the feta and toss to combine. Season lightly with salt and pepper then cover and refrigerate until ready to serve.

4.  Pour the other half of the vinaigrette mixture into a large bowl and stir in half the yogurt until well combined. Add the cubed chicken and turn several times to coat well.

5.  Thread the chicken cubes onto metal skewers.

6.  Reduce the heat of the grill to medium them grill the chicken for about 5 minutes (for charcoal grill) or 10 minutes (for gas grill), or until the internal temperature of the chicken reaches 160 degrees F.

7.  Carefully remove the chicken from the skewers and transfer to serving plates. Spoon the salad on the side. Add a dollop of the remaining yogurt to the side then serve right away.

# Oven Roasted Chicken Thighs with Fennel, Orange and Olive Sauce

*Number of Servings: 6*

*Cooking and Preparation Time: 1 hour*

## Ingredients:

- 6 bone-in chicken thighs, 6 oz. each
- 2 shallots, thinly sliced
- 1 anchovy fillet, rinsed
- 1/3 cup chopped fresh flat leaf parsley
- 4 Tbsp. chopped pitted oil cured black olives
- 3 Tbsp. extra virgin olive oil
- 3 Tbsp. water
- 1 ½ tsp. red wine vinegar
- 1 tsp. freshly grated orange zest
- 1/3 tsp. ground fennel seeds
- Red pepper flakes, to taste
- Sea salt, to taste
- Freshly ground black pepper, to taste

## How to Prepare:

1. First prepare the sauce by combining the parsley, shallots, water, olives, vinegar, orange zest, fennel seeds, a dash of red pepper

flakes, and a pinch of salt in a food processor. Cover and process until smooth.

2. Gradually drizzle in the olive oil as you process until the mixture is well incorporated. Set aside.

3. Set the oven to 450 degrees F to preheat.

4. Place one oven rack on the lowest section and place a rimmed baking sheet on top to catch the drippings. Place the second rack on top of the lower one.

5. Rinse the chicken thighs then blot dry with paper towels. Poke all over with a sharp knife and then rub with olive oil all over. Season with salt and pepper.

6. Cut out 12 x 12 inches of aluminium foil and place the chicken thighs on top, then place another sheet of aluminium foil. Crimp the edges to seal.

7. Place the packet of chicken thighs in the oven on the upper rack and roast the chicken thighs for 25 minutes, rotating after the first 12 minutes. Once the internal temperature of the chicken thigh is 160 degrees F, it is ready.

8. Take the packet of chicken out of the oven and then set the oven to broil.

9. Carefully remove the chicken from the packet then broil for 5 minutes to make the skin crisp and brown. Then, transfer to a serving dish.

10. Pour the sauce into a gravy boat and serve alongside the roasted chicken. Best served right away.

# Oven Roasted Chicken Thighs with Moroccan Style Currant and Pistachio Sauce

*Number of Servings: 6*

*Cooking and Preparation Time: 1 hour*

## Ingredients:

- 6 bone-in chicken thighs, 6 oz. each
- 2 shallots, thinly sliced
- 1/3 cup chopped fresh flat leaf parsley
- 4 Tbsp. water
- 4 Tbsp. dried currants
- 4 Tbsp. toasted shelled pistachios
- 3 Tbsp. extra virgin olive oil
- ¾ Tbsp. freshly squeezed lime juice
- 1/3 tsp. ground cinnamon
- ¼ tsp. orange blossom water
- Sea salt, to taste
- Freshly ground black pepper, to taste

## How to Prepare:

11. First prepare the sauce by combining the parsley, shallots, currants, water, pistachios, lime juice, orange blossom water, cinnamon, and a pinch of salt in a food processor. Cover and process until smooth.

12. Gradually drizzle in the olive oil as you process until the mixture is well incorporated. Set aside.
13. Set the oven to 450 degrees F to preheat.
14. Place one oven rack on the lowest section and place a rimmed baking sheet on top to catch the drippings. Place the second rack on top of the lower one.
15. Rinse the chicken thighs then blot dry with paper towels. Poke all over with a sharp knife and then rub with olive oil all over. Season with salt and pepper.
16. Cut out 12 x 12 inches of aluminium foil and place the chicken thighs on top, then place another sheet of aluminium foil. Crimp the edges to seal.
17. Place the packet of chicken thighs in the oven on the upper rack and roast the chicken thighs for 25 minutes, rotating after the first 12 minutes. Once the internal temperature of the chicken thigh is 160 degrees F, it is ready.
18. Take the packet of chicken out of the oven and then set the oven to broil.
19. Carefully remove the chicken from the packet then broil for 5 minutes to make the skin crisp and brown. Then, transfer to a serving dish.
20. Pour the sauce into a gravy boat and serve alongside the roasted chicken. Best served right away.

# Chicken Saute with Romesco Sauce

*Number of Servings: 2*

*Cooking and Preparation Time: 45 minutes*

## Ingredients:

- 2 boneless, skinless chicken breasts, 6 oz. each
- 2 tsp. extra virgin olive oil
- Sea salt, to taste
- Freshly ground black pepper, to taste

*For the Sauce:*

- 1 garlic clove, peeled and sliced thinly
- ½ cup jarred roasted red pepper, rinsed and blotted dry with paper towels
- ¼ slice white bread, shredded
- 2 Tbsp. toasted hazelnuts
- 1 Tbsp. extra virgin olive oil
- ¾ Tbsp. sherry vinegar
- ½ tsp. honey
- ¼ tsp. smoked paprika
- ¼ tsp. sea salt
- Cayenne pepper, to taste

**How to Prepare:**

1. Prepare the sauce by combining the bread, hazelnuts, and ½ tablespoon olive oil into a wide skillet over medium flame. Stir until toasted.
2. Add the garlic and stir until fragrant, then transfer to a food processor and process until finely shredded.
3. Add the red pepper, honey, vinegar, paprika, cayenne, remaining olive oil and salt. Cover and blend until finely ground. Pour the mixture into a bowl and set aside.
4. Place the chicken breasts between two sheets of plastic wrap and lay on a flat hard surface. Gently pound on them until flat, then blot dry with paper towels.
5. Season the chicken with salt and pepper then set aside.
6. Wipe the skillet clean and place over medium-high flame. Once hot, add half the olive oil and swirl to coat.
7. Cook the chicken in batches until browned all over, about 2 minutes per side. Then, transfer to a serving dish and spoon the Romesco sauce on top. Best served right away.

# Spicy Moroccan Lamb and Lentil Stew

*Number of Servings: 4*

*Cooking and Preparation Time: 1 hour and 30 minutes*

## Ingredients:

- ½ lb. lamb shoulder chops, trimmed and halved
- 2 plum tomatoes, chopped
- 1 small onion, peeled and diced
- 5 cups chicken broth
- 1/3 cup brown or green lentils, rinsed thoroughly
- 3 Tbsp. chopped fresh cilantro
- 2 ½ Tbsp. harissa
- ½ Tbsp. extra virgin olive oil
- ½ Tbsp. whole wheat flour
- ½ tsp. freshly grated ginger
- ½ tsp. ground cumin
- ¼ tsp. paprika
- Ground cinnamon, to taste
- Cayenne pepper, to taste
- Sea salt, to taste
- Freshly ground black pepper, to taste

## How to Prepare:

1. Set the oven to 325 degrees F to preheat.
2. Rinse the lamb and then blot dry with paper towels. Season all over with salt and pepper then set aside.
3. Place an ovenproof stock pot over medium-high flame and heat through. Once hot, add the olive oil and swirl to coat. Add the lamb and brown all over, about 4 minutes per side. Then, transfer to a platter and set aside.
4. Drain most of the fat from the stock pot except for 1 tablespoon. Reheat over medium low flame and sauté the onion until translucent.
5. Add the ginger, paprika, cumin, cinnamon, cayenne, saffron threads, and black pepper. Sauté until fragrant, then add the flour and sauté until combined.
6. Gradually stir in the broth and scrape up the browned bits in the pot. Increase heat and bring to a boil, then reduce to a simmer.
7. Place the lamb back into the stock pot along with the juices. Bring to a simmer, then cover and cook for about 10 minutes.
8. Add the lentils and chickpeas then cover and transfer the pot to the preheated oven. Cook for 1 hour, or until the lamb is tender.
9. Transfer the lamb to a chopping board and then slice into bite-sized pieces. Discard the bones and excess fat.
10. Place the sliced lamb back into the soup and stir well to combine. Reheat over low flame and stir in the tomatoes, harissa, cilantro, and a dash of salt and pepper to taste. Ladle into individual bowls and serve. Best served right away.

# Libyan Lamb and Mint Sharba

*Number of Servings: 4*

*Cooking and Preparation Time: 45 minutes*

## Ingredients:

- ½ lb. lamb shoulder chops, trimmed and halved
- 1 small onion, peeled and chopped
- 2 plum tomatoes, chopped
- 7.5 oz. canned chickpeas, rinsed thoroughly
- 5 cups chicken broth
- ½ cup orzo
- 1 Tbsp. tomato paste
- ½ Tbsp. extra virgin olive oil
- ¾ tsp. crumbled dried mint
- ½ tsp. paprika
- ½ tsp. ground turmeric
- ¼ tsp. ground cinnamon
- Ground cumin, to taste
- Sea salt, to taste
- Freshly ground black pepper, to taste

**How to Prepare:**

1. Set the oven to 325 degrees F to preheat.
2. Rinse the lamb thoroughly then blot dry with paper towels. Season all over with salt and pepper and set aside.
3. Place an ovenproof stock pot over medium-high flame and heat through. Once hot, add the olive oil and swirl to coat. Add the lamb and brown all over, about 4 minutes per side. Then, transfer to a platter and set aside.
4. Drain most of the fat from the stock pot except for 1 tablespoon. Reheat over medium low flame and sauté the onion until translucent.
5. Add the tomatoes and sauté until tender, then add the tomato paste, turmeric, paprika, cinnamon, cumin, a pinch of salt and pepper, and ½ teaspoon of mint. Stir well until fragrant.
6. Gradually stir in the broth and scrape up the browned bits in the pot. Increase heat and bring to a boil, then reduce to a simmer.
7. Stir in the chickpeas then place the lamb back into the stock pot along with the juices. Bring to a simmer, then cover and cook for about 1 hour, or until the lamb is tender.
8. Transfer the lamb to a chopping board and then shred the meat. Discard the bones and excess fat.
9. Place the shredded lamb back into the soup and stir well to combine. Reheat over low flame and stir in the reserved mint. Ladle into individual bowls and serve. Best served right away.

# Chapter 8 – Snacks and Light Meals

## Pita Bread

*Number of Servings: 12 (1 pita bread per serving)*

*Cooking and Preparation Time: 1 hour, with 2 hours and 30 minutes resting time for the dough*

### Ingredients:

- 30 oz. bread flour
- 1 ¾ cups water, at room temperature
- 1/3 cup extra virgin olive oil
- 3 ½ tsp. rapid rise yeast
- 3 ½ tsp. sugar
- 3 tsp. sea salt

### How to Prepare:

1. In a large bowl, whisk together the yeast, flour, and salt using an electric mixer.
2. In a measuring cup, combine the sugar, water, and olive oil and whisk well until the sugar is dissolved.
3. Attach the dough hook to the electric mixer then set to low. Gradually mix the sugar oil mixture into the flour mixture until

a dough starts to form. Continue to knead with the electric mixer until the dough becomes elastic and smooth.

4. Lightly grease a large bowl and set aside.
5. Lightly flour a clean flat surface and add the dough. Shape into a smooth ball then place in the prepared bowl. Cover with plastic wrap and set aside to let the dough rise for about 2 hours.
6. After 2 hours, punch down on the dough to deflate and then transfer to a lightly floured surface. Divide into six pieces, then divide each peace in half. Cover again with plastic.
7. Take one piece of dough from underneath the plastic at a time and shape into a ball. Then, stretch out and smoothen. Dredge the ball in flour and place on the floured surface. Then, shape into an 8 inch round piece and cover with plastic. Repeat with the remaining dough balls then let rest for about 20 minutes.
8. At least an hour before baking, set the oven rack to the lower middle section and place the baking stone on top. Set the oven to 500 degrees F to preheat.
9. Flour a baking sheet and add 2 dough rounds. Place the rounds on the baking stone and bake for 1 minute, or until an air pocket starts to form. Flip over the pita breads and bake for another 1 minute. Transfer to a plate and cover to keep warm. Repeat with the remaining dough balls.
10. Store the pita bread in an airtight container on a cool shelf for up to 3 days, in the refrigerator for up to 1 week, or the freezer for up to 1 month. Reheat before serving.

# Savory Chickpea Flatbread

*Number of Servings: 8*

*Cooking and Preparation Time: 30 minutes*

## Ingredients:

- 2 cups chickpea flour
- 2 cups water
- ½ cup extra virgin olive oil
- ¾ tsp. turmeric
- ¾ tsp. sea salt
- ¾ tsp. freshly ground black pepper

## How to Prepare:

1. Set the oven rack to the middle section. Set the oven to 200 degrees F to preheat.
2. Place a wire rack with a rimmed baking sheet on the oven.
3. Combine the chickpea flour, salt, and pepper in a bowl. Stir in the turmeric and mix well.
4. Gradually stir the water into the chickpea flour mixture then mix in 4 ½ tablespoons of olive oil. Mix well until smooth.
5. Place a skillet over medium-high flame and heat through. Once hot, add 2 teaspoons of oil and swirl to coat.
6. Add ½ cup of the chickpea batter onto the skillet and tilt to create a flat, even pancake. Reduce to medium low flame and cook for 3 minutes or until the edges are golden brown and crisp.

7. Flip the bread over and cook for an added 1 minute. Transfer to the wire rack inside the oven to keep warm.
8. Repeat with the remaining batter and olive oil. Best served warm.

# Spanish Chili Garlic Mushrooms

*Number of Servings: 3*

*Cooking and Preparation Time: 20 minutes*

## Ingredients:

- ½ lb. small button mushrooms, chopped
- 2 large garlic cloves, peeled and slivered
- ½ small dried chilli pepper, chopped
- ¼ cup low sodium chicken or beef broth
- 2 ½ Tbsp. chopped fresh flat leaf parsley
- ½ Tbsp. extra virgin olive oil
- ½ Tbsp. freshly squeezed lemon juice

## How to Prepare:

1. Place a saucepan over low flame and add the olive oil. Swirl to coat, then stir in the garlic and chilli. Simmer, stirring frequently, for 3 minutes or until the garlic is golden.
2. Stir the mushrooms into the pan and sauté until tender and heated through. Season to taste with salt.
3. Increase to medium flame then pour in the broth. Stir well, then loosely cover and simmer for 7 minutes or until the mushrooms are completely tender.
4. Add the lemon juice and parsley then simmer for 2 minutes, or until the parsley is wilted.
5. Transfer to a serving bowl. May be served warm or chilled.

# Goat Cheese and Roasted Bell Pepper Dip

*Number of Servings: 6*

*Cooking and Preparation Time: 5 minutes*

## Ingredients:

- 3 large roasted red bell peppers in olive oil, drained and chopped
- ¾ cup fresh goat cheese
- 1 Tbsp. extra virgin olive oil
- 1 tsp. freshly squeezed lemon juice
- Sea salt, to taste
- Freshly ground black pepper, to taste

## How to Prepare:

1. Combine the bell peppers and goat cheese in the food processor, then add the lemon juice and olive oil. Cover and pulse until smooth.
2. Season to taste with salt and pepper then blend again to combine.
3. Transfer the dip to a bowl, cover, and refrigerate for up to 2 days. Best served chilled with fresh vegetable sticks.

# Green Olive and Lentil Dip

*Number of Servings:  5 (1 ¼ cups)*

*Cooking and Preparation Time: 5 minutes*

## Ingredients:

- 1 garlic clove, peeled and crushed
- 1 ¼ cups Greek green olives, pitted, rinsed and drained
- ¼ cup cooked green lentils, drained
- 1 ½ Tbsp. freshly squeezed lemon juice
- 1 Tbsp. extra virgin olive oil
- ½ Tbsp. blanched almonds
- 1 tsp. freshly grated lemon zest
- Sea salt, to taste
- Freshly ground white pepper, to taste
- Chopped fresh dill, to taste

## How to Prepare:

1. Combine the lemon juice, almonds and garlic in a food processor and process until the almonds are chopped.
2. Pour in the olives and process until chopped as well, then pour in the lentils and pulse until crushed, but not mashed.
3. Pour the mixture into a serving bowl, then stir in the lemon zest. Sprinkle with salt, pepper, and dill, then drizzle the olive oil on top.

4. Serve the dip right away or chilled, with whole grain bread sticks or vegetable sticks.

# Conclusion

Hopefully this book has inspired you to stick to the Mediterranean diet as well as prepare delicious and healthy home-cooked meals on a regular basis. Continue to make your own meal plans and maintain a wonderfully well-stocked kitchen so you will never run out of ideas and motivation.

Also, do not be afraid to explore even more Mediterranean dishes and to try to recreate them in your own kitchen. In fact, you should not hesitate to invite family and friends to join you in preparing your meals in the kitchen. Another thing that makes the Mediterranean lifestyle unique and interesting is that it acknowledges the importance of friendship and family, so have fun sharing the meals and the time in preparing them.

CPSIA information can be obtained
at www.ICGtesting.com
Printed in the USA
LVHW050516070221
678613LV00043B/878

9 781979 237666